A Vo;ce For The Vo;celess

Ben Sanchez

A Vo;ce For The Vo;celess © 2023

Ben Sanchez

All rights reserved.

Presentation by *BookLeaf Publishing*

Web: www.bookleafpub.com

E-mail: info@bookleafpub.com

ISBN: 9789358312232

First edition 2023

To Angelica Urbina, whose brilliant mind and poetic challenges have shaped the very essence of my artistry. Your intellectual prowess and unwavering support have propelled my creativity to new heights, forever weaving intricate tapestries of thought and expression.

To Glorymar Santiago, my unwavering champion and steadfast admirer, your unwavering belief in my work has been a constant source of inspiration. Your encouragement fuels my passion, guiding me through the labyrinth of words, as I paint vivid landscapes of emotion and meaning.

And to my beloved grandmother, Alicia Melendez, whose absence is felt deeply but whose spirit resides within every word I pen. You ignited the spark of storytelling in my soul, infusing my veins with the ink of imagination. Your legacy lives on, forever guiding my quill as I honor your memory through the power of written verse.

May this dedication serve as a testament to the profound impact each of you has had on my poetic journey. With gratitude and love, I offer this book as a tribute to the unbreakable bonds that shape me as a writer and as a person.

ACKNOWLEDGEMENT

To all who have contributed to the creation and realization of "A Voice For The Voiceless," I extend my deepest gratitude. Your support, encouragement, and inspiration have made this project possible.

My heartfelt thanks go to my family for their unwavering support and belief in my artistic endeavors. Your love and encouragement have fueled my creative journey.

I am grateful to Josef Desade for his wisdom, expertise, and dedication to the craft of writing. Your influence will forever resonate in my words. To Rebbeca Morin, thank you for introducing me to Dead on a Doorstep and providing a space for my voice to flourish.

A special acknowledgment goes to Luke Beckwith, my co-writer and editor, for his enthusiasm, constructive feedback, and genuine appreciation of my work. Your commitment to excellence and attention to detail have transformed my words into a tangible form that I am proud to share.

I dedicate this collection to the voiceless souls whose stories, struggles, and triumphs have inspired these poems. It is for you that I write, hoping your voices will be heard and your experiences will find solace within these pages.

Lastly, I thank Black Noise for their profound impact on shaping the themes and narratives of this poetry book.

To each and every one of you, thank you for being a part of this journey. Your presence has left an indelible mark on my heart, and I am forever grateful for your support, love, and belief in me.

With deepest appreciation,
Ben Sanchez (Icarus)

PREFACE

Dear poetry lovers,
I am thrilled to introduce my debut poetry book. My writing process is guided by a deep-seated aspiration to make a positive difference in the world and establish genuine connections with people through their stories. By giving voice to the voiceless, I aim to bring these topics to the forefront and illuminate their significance.

My poetry collection is a tapestry of the human experience, interwoven with delicate nuances and hidden truths that dwell within the shadows. Each poem stands independently, yet they are interwoven to form a larger narrative, offering glimpses into the universal human experience. It is my sincerest desire that this collection resonates with you, ignites meaningful conversations, and fosters connections that transcend the boundaries of time and space.

I am honored to have gained the attention and admiration of those who have become fans of my work. To you, the reader, I express my utmost intentions. May this collection resonate with you on a profound level, evoking emotions and contemplation. May it serve as a testament to the power of words, reminding you that you are never alone, and your voice is heard.

In closing, I extend my sincerest gratitude to all those who have supported me throughout the creation of this poetry collection. I am humbled and honored to share this collection with you, and it is my sincerest hope that it touches your soul and leaves an indelible mark.

With heartfelt appreciation,

Ben Sanchez (Icarus)

The Truth of Prometheus

Whispers of the past, come forth,
Let us explore what lays within the shadows.
The fury ignited in this candle of mine,
Once a gentle glow, now untamed hellfire,
A wildfire raging, directionless.
Sowing wanton destruction.
A meteor shower, once softly blazing through
the velvet night,
Now raining havoc from the heavens.
As my heart quivers in fear,
The damage done, irreversible,
Fated to endless pain, like Prometheus chained
to his mountain.
My good deeds have never gone unpunished.

Let us explore these ripples, and sink beneath
their waves.
Eyes once alight with joy, now clouded,
Emotions surge like tidal waves,
Innocence submerged, bravery forced,
My soul quickly succumbs to the darkness.
Listen with me to the voices, whispering of days
long since passed,
Lamenting the path we've taken,

Blind to the shattered remnants of youth,
Never absolved of the consequences of my
mistakes,
The blame, heavy upon my shoulders.

So let my pen strike true,
A meteor streaking across the soft velvet of
paper,
Words raining down like celestial arrows amidst
a medieval battlefield,
An unrelenting inferno, white hot anger burning
all to ash.

Together, we'll release the tears,
An ocean of sorrow and lost memories, echoing
back from easier times,
A tidal wave washing away deceit,
The naive reality they embrace.
So cast your stones upon us,
Blame us for speaking our truth,

Portrayed as monsters for living the truth, and
inking our stories upon paper.
Cast into the gutter for refusing to hide in fear
amongst the sheep.

Fragments of a Broken Heart

You made them main characters of your story,
Believing their words would echo through
eternity,
Idealizing a version of them,
Your heart's delusion, a twisted reality.

But ideals are seldom pure,
And now you lie shattered, broken,
Like glass fragments scattered on the floor,
Confused, lost, and unspoken.

Memories are shackles that drag,
Binding you to a past self,
Like antique traps in a forgotten storage.

Their laughter echoes in your head,
A malevolent sound that twists,
A darkness that threatens to drown,
Dragging you down with its fists.

Silence suffocates with its weight,
Leaving you shattered, confined,
A reminder of all that's lost,
And the thought of peace scares your mind.

You fear the unknown cast,
Yet you welcome death's embrace,
Regardless of the fear it holds,
Or the unknown that awaits.

All you want is to let go,
For the pain and memories are too much to bear,
A weight you can no longer carry,
A burden you cannot share.

Your heart lies shattered, your soul in pain,
The memories of love now a bittersweet stain,
A story of heartbreak, a tale of woe,
A tragedy that only you can know.

But know this, dear heart, you are not alone,
For others have felt the pain you've known,
And though it may seem like the end,
This heartbreak is just the beginning, my friend.

For in the broken pieces of your heart,
There lies a strength that will set you apart,
A resilience that will carry you through,
And a love that will one day be renewed.

So let the tears fall, let the pain be felt,
For in these moments, true healing is dealt,
And though the road may be long and hard,
Know that you will mend, dear heart.

May these words paint a picture in your mind,
Of a heart that's broken, a soul that's blind,
May they evoke the pain that you feel,
And help you heal, and help you deal.

The Devil in the Suit

Your world was set ablaze,
And in the midst of the conflagration,
You embraced a beguiling foe in a suit,
A portal that you would ruefully lament
unsealing.

You bartered your essence for a solitary
osculation,
A reckless yearning that bore a ponderous toll.
Yet, akin to a devotee, you eschewed the
portents
And reveled in the euphoria you imbibed in his
aura.

As a flagellant, you craved his pernicious
affection.
Malignantly, he eviscerated your core,
Marooning you at the celestial gates,
Like detritus hurtling towards an abyss.

As all succumbed to stygian darkness,
You descended from the empyrean-like
fulmination
Poised to assail the terra firma.

You repose here on the loam, encircled by
withered roses,
Gradually hemorrhaging, pining for his ardor.
Only to extend your grasp for him,
As he evanesced into the penumbra, never to
reappear.

Boundless Cage

Delicate butterfly,
Wings of fragile stained glass,
Pierced by a malevolent force,
Desirous of rendering you insignificant.

Harsh blows echo,
Eliciting cries of deep-seated anguish,
As you crawl, yearning for sanctuary,
Yet, all you can muster is to relinquish hope and
Endure.

Your frail form etched with hues of black and
Purple,
A grotesque testament to malignant supremacy.
Your heart harbored a simple yearning,
To love and be loved,
Yet, you were rewarded with lacerated lips and
Contusions,
A cruel homage to such a pure aspiration.

Now you tremble as you strive towards the
heavens,
Tears cascading, imploring the divine to halt this
Insanity,
No longer able to bear the whispers of your

Tormentors,
Or the ceaseless dread of the palpable reminders
of
The atrocities committed.

Tragically, in the end, you lie there, devoid of
life,
Your gaze fixed on the vast expanse of sky,
A boundless cage,
An incessant reminder of the trauma that has
Relentlessly shackled you.

Post Traumatic Survival Disorder

My mind is a barren warzone,
Marred and torn by the constant struggle for
survival that has been my life to this point.
A battle that has left me scarred,
And robbed me of my innocence.

My emotions are bottled up inside me,
And my wounds bleed on every page,
As I try to right the wrongs of my past,
But the screams of agony and despair remain.

The trauma I've endured has nearly extinguished
The light within my heart,
And left me struggling to find my worth,
Lost and alone in a world that constantly sends
me spiraling into flashbacks.

There's no escape from this endless nightmare,
No relief from the pain and suffering that I
endure.
The horrors of my past haunt me every day,
And the world around me is a constant trigger.

The darkness consumes me,

And I'm angry at every sound,
Every careless word that enters my ears,
Adding to the chaos that surrounds me.

I lay there wasting the days away,
Feeling like my soul is forever trapped,
Unable to find a way out of this darkness,
And unable to see the light at the end of the
tunnel.

In this battle for survival,
I'm left with nothing but despair,
As I struggle to make sense of the pain,
And find a way to heal the wounds
That have left me broken and scared.

Winter Dreams

O' my fellow poet,
How I watch you quiver like the naked trees in
the icy wind,
As you struggle with your tired eyes,
The twilight and evening bell of the altar rings,
Tolling out its harsh directives into the soft
snowy countryside.

While you lay in your tundra prison,
Slowly painting the frigid pale sheet from soft
ivory to dark crimson,
I watch, as your eyes well with tears that carry
away your body's last reserves of heat,
Listening to you quietly whisper your final
words of comfort.

Unfortunately, your time has come,
Your clock has struck the point of no return,
So dream away to the times of winter festivities,
Of a time where the rum tasted like sweet
Nirvana,
Back to the times where darkness was never to
be found in your heart,
Only the burning passion of love and tranquility,

The astounding and profound wonder of what
lay in the wintery night.

So breathe out your last words on this winter
solstice,
As I hold your hand and you depart to your
afterlife of sombre slumber,
Don't let fear take safe harbour in your soul a
moment longer,
For there is nothing left to fear.

Let us say goodbye and live an eternity in
whatever afterlife awaits,
And dream once more, of Winter.

His Darker Truth

Throughout the changing scenes of life,
Death, like a stubborn specter, clung to your heel
as a shackle.
Until this moment, this profound instant.

Your armaments, pledged to protect both
yourself and those beloved souls,
Stand silent, impotent beside the newest casualty
of war.
The crimson life already pooling,
Staining the cold earth beneath your soles,

Somehow, this vision surpasses the horror
you've previously known.
The dreadful tableau gradually gains clarity - the
lifeless face belongs to your closest comrade.

A blackout descends, mingling seething anger,
raw denial, and unrefined rage within it.
You see, as if stuck in time, your bullets rending
his murderer to shreds.

Yet, this vengeance, so pure, so primal, attracted
scorn,

And for that transgression, you're banished to
the nether realms.
Imprisoned in Tartarus' dreadful pits,
Condemned in this hellish deep for their
senseless war's sins.

The world, once familiar, turns its frigid
shoulder,
Sunshine from the heavens refuses to bestow its
warmth upon you.

Regrettably, it was those very bullets that
seduced with deceptive pledges.
Now, you remain bound here,
Immersed in a sea of your potent liquor and
interred beneath a flurry of white purity.

The Reckoning of Secrets

In the shadows, darkness looms,
A force too strong to fight,
Born of a life lived in sin,
You crumble, begging for the light.
The Reckoning of Secrets

Sins too dark to reveal,
You yearn for liberation,
But pride and guilt consume your soul,
And you face your condemnation.

The voices of guilt persist,
Like savage beasts they tear,
Devouring your final moments,
As death looms near.

Your thirst for life's sweetest wine,
Has led you to this end,
Now you face your reckoning,
For all the secrets you've kept penned.

A Silent Goodbye

With fists bloodied, our fate's pages stained,
Ensnared in a shadowed prison, trauma
unexplained.
The dormant creature awakens with a bellow,
Kneeling for solace, yearning for respite's glow.
Beseeching aid to halt this perpetual quest,
Yet reason succumbs, swallowed by eternal
night's crest.

With labored breath and weary eyes' gaze,
Thunder's rumble entreats for a tender embrace.
Where icy winds freeze your vulnerable core,
Your truths unveiled fall on deaf ears, ignored.
Embracing poison in the waning hour's tread,
To silence echoes that leave your soul
threadbare.

As the church bell chimes, your essence takes
flight,
A bittersweet smile, serenity ignites your sight.
But your tranquil departure awakens screams,
Loved ones pleading for your return from
dreams.

Haunted by Regret

Within the realm of loving you, I find regret,
For offering my heart, my truth, with no safety
net,
Naivety beckoned me towards your web of lies,
A mirage of touch, a disguise before my eyes.

In solemn depths, my sanity was consumed,
A toll extracted, leaving my spirit entombed,
Robbing me of self-worth, numbing my soul's
core,
A loveless tether, an empty hearth I deplore.

Now, at 1 am, I find solace in whiskey's
embrace,
Three shots searing, framing your lips' tainted
grace,
Seeking to drown memories and sins so profane,
Intertwined within each sip, a futile attempt to
restrain.

The room cloaked in dimness, heavy air laced
with smoke,
Its sharp scent choking, evoking memories, a
cruel joke,
The clinking of ice echoes in a glass's grasp,

An ode to haunting memories, refusing to lapse.

Yet they persist, misery and pain, unrelenting
foes,
Ghostly reminders of the past's relentless throes,
A burden I bear, without knowing self-love's
worth,
A cross I carry, longing for a renewal of my
rebirth.

The Scars Of Icarus

Your heart screams out to the sun,
Begging for its warm embrace once more,
And though you cried for salvation to the
heavens,
Your prayer was ignored by the gods,
Not even Apollo answered your cries,
For you were Icarus in this story,
The child who flew too close to the burning sun,
And fell from the heavens.

Crashing into the sea,
engulfed in loneliness and darkness.
Now an empty void exists within your chest,
Love no longer tucks you in,
Sweet dreams no longer linger upon your
waking mind.
Only the horrors that your matriarch has
bestowed
in your soul, while her counterpart watches in
silence.

Now you lay there, your flesh tainted by men's
hands,
Only to fill the void of love that you were never
given.

A temporary fix to mend those scars that were
given to you
by the woman who conceived you.
In the end you put all these scars on your skin
for all of those who never stay,
For these scars on your arms
bely your truth.

The Crown of Regret

Our villain stumbles through a hall of broken
glass,
His drunken stagger threatening to knock
his crown from its perch
Lost in a sea of nameless, faceless dread,
He's haunted by the specters of his past
betrayals.
Mired in a web of bitter lies and deceit, he thinks
back upon his lost dreams of paradise,
Laying beneath the moon with his love.

Yet now he has become a prisoner of his own
illusions,
and thereof,
A victim of his own deceit and pride.
The world he knew has crumbled into dust,
 a result of his past transgressions.
And he lies gazing at the shadow of his home,
A distant memory now lost to rust,
A fading dream that he can no longer revive.

He gave too much to those that only took,
A heart of darkness hidden behind
a masterfully crafted disguise.
But now he is nothing but a deceitful crook,

ensnared in his own web,
A king without right laid to rest beneath
the moon's cold gaze.

The crown of villainous kings weighs heavy on
his brow,
A symbol of the power and corruption that he's
sown,
A burden he shall never be absolved of,
A legacy of darkness left to be atoned for by
generations that follow.

Death's Shot Glass

The cork clatters to the ground as your final
shred of hope splashes into the skull shot glass,
Your last bit of faith tossed aside.
You seal your fate with a solemn vow.
A life sentence you thought would bring relief,
A silent goodbye.

You believed that your quiet exit would benefit
the world,
That you would stop needlessly occupying
needed space.
As you slowly fade into the encroaching
darkness, you are surprised by the wave of panic
that fills the room.
They rush you to the bathroom, hoping they can
save you from the poison beginning to course
through your system.

Watching you slowly open your eyes, tears
streaming down your face,
Regretting every shot you took,
You're begging for forgiveness, water droplets
raining over you in the shower.
Although they tell you that everything will be
alright,
They fail to see the naivety of those words.

Time slowly passes, and you continue to spiral.
Your hope for life dwindles into nothingness.
As your soul slowly turns to dust, you cling to
that bottle of poison,
Watching as its contents drain into your
stomach, eating away at the remnants of your
being like hot acid.

You feel hollow, empty, like a mannequin left
standing lifelessly,
Grotesquely posed, a shell of what you once
were, consumed by your own darkness.
It's been so long since you left this world,
But the sound of your shot glass as it hit the
floor shall echo through my skull for eternity.

A haunting reminder of the day you chose to end
it all,
To look death in the eye and embrace it.
There was no obituary written for your passing,
No wake, no burial, no one to mourn your loss.
The ones who spoke those words of reassurance
were nowhere to be found,
Leaving you to face your fate alone and
forgotten.

And yet, as the world keeps turning, you remain,

A ghost of your former self, wandering
aimlessly,
Haunted by the memories of what could have
been.
Of the life that slipped away, beyond your grasp.

To the world, you were a villain,
A wretched creature deserving of nothing but
contempt and scorn.
But to me, you were a fallen angel, cast out from
heaven,
Shunned by the holy men who claimed to know
the truth.

You were my winged friend, my confidant,
The only one who truly saw me for who I am.
But as time passed, our bond grew twisted and
dark,
A toxic obsession that consumed us both.

And now you're gone, lost to the abyss,
Fallen like Icarus, tumbling into the darkness
below.
But unlike him, you did not crash into the
ocean's depths,
Instead, you descended into the depths of your
own despair.

Now you lie there, a corpse on your throne,

A testament to the darkness that consumed you
whole.
And though I mourn for what we could have
been,
I know that your end was inevitable, a tragedy
foretold.

Vultures

Tonight I endure this burden
of watching as you lay there like a corpse,
A horrifying sight I never thought I would
witness beneath the sunset.

Covered in scratches and scars from the vultures
that
devoured what was left of your carcass.
Time had no patience for you,
No qualms with your suffering,
It was only eager to wipe you from existence
like paint over canvas.
Now you lay still on my arm as the last light of
day
fades into the horizon,
Slowly sinking as you slip away from me.

I'm paralyzed,
This horrid moment life has forced me to
witness dragging onwards.
These voices imprisoned me in this unwanted
hellscape,
Constantly reminding me of the failure I've
become for not
being your salvation.

Now I fall on my knees,
As time watches me become lifeless just so
these vultures
can feed on my heart as I collapse lifeless next
to you.

Forgotten Oath

You claimed your love for her was
unconditional,
You were supposed to love her, as she lay in her
cradle,
Eyes opening for the very first time.

In time, she blossomed into a gorgeous maiden,
And yet, still you forgot your role as parents.
You suffocate the life out of her and
Naively call it love.

And when she screams and shouts her truth,
You silence her by putting her beneath you.

And even so, even after all her heartache,
She finally broke out of the iron shackles you
Placed on her.

Even when her voice echoed to the heavens,
You tried to tug upon the strings of fate like you
were some grotesque, twisted
Puppeteer of her life.

Fortunately, your ignorant words will
No longer work on her.

There are no cries for wolf,
Nor lies that will deceive her.

So lay in your bed of thorns,
For your ignorance has cast her
Into the gaping maw of the unknown,
All because you have forgotten your oath
As parents.

Death's Cold Brew

Don't let those sirens come upon my sanctum,
Painstakingly built upon the old bones,
harvested from the corpse of the man I once
was.
Deafen my ears to these demons,
that lurk amongst
the shadows I once recognized as home.
Where they once enslaved me, forced to walk
the path they paved for me.

A path where my heart never knew peace,
But rather grew accustomed to the malice these
demons harbored in their cold, black hearts.
Hear my pleading heart divine patriarch,
Pull me away from this path that has thus sullied
my work,
A path where death once handed me a tall glass,
Filled to the brim with poison and ill intent
Cage the beast that yearns to be free of its
warden,
Lock away that hatred, which so patiently awaits
the chance to tear my safe haven asunder,
Obliterating all that I love and hold dear,
All that protects me from your cloying evil.

Burn all the ropes that crave the feeling of
alighting around my neck,
For my heart fears to flourish and expose its
innermost truths, and wishes to know the
grimmest fate,
Before all the good comes to flourish in my
home.
So save me from The firing squad,
For their bullets spell catastrophe, meant to
silence my light,
And devour what good works I have wrought
before me.

Celestial Love Unbound

In the sanctuary of her heart,
a profound love, dwarfing the vast sea,
overlooked, her infinite gifts remain,
boundless love, sustained in silence.

Her heart, as vast as night,
an ocean of love, enduring, infinite.
In return, a stream so slight,
bound in twilight's lament.

Love, a celestial force,
governed by the moon's quiet course,
eclipsed, whispered secrets to the cold,
a healer's touch, undervalued, untold.

Love's tempest met with apathy's chill,
in her heart, no resentment, only goodwill.
Longing for acknowledgment, wishing for
contentment,
a love story lost in the cosmos's infinite moment.

A tale of sorrow,
a maiden who loved deeper than the world could
borrow,
a testament to a love unseen,
unreturned, untamed, forever free.

Four Seasons of Grief

Beside the window, you linger, day and night,
Yearning to join her on her voyage to the
unknown,
But destiny has etched its unyielding course,
And solitude remains, my cherished friend.

Spring's promise of renewal now bears a taint,
The acrid sting of sorrow and despair,
As you witness life's resurgence from dormancy,
While she abides, eternally adrift, irreparable.

Summer's tender warmth now feels glacial,
A stark reminder of the void within your heart,
Longing for her caress, her voice, her laughter,
Yet only echoes of her departure persist.

Autumn's vivid hues appear to taunt you,
Their incandescent shades a brutal memento of
the past,
As you meander without aim through the
dimming light,
Marooned in a realm devoid of her, without
purpose.

Winter's frost offers the sole solace you find,

As you seek refuge in the biting gales,
A reminder of her skin's icy touch,
An essence you cannot grasp, cannot revoke.

You linger, petrified by the recollection of her
farewell,
Praying it was naught but a ghastly dream,
But the truth is an unrelenting reality you cannot
flee,
As the burden of your loss overwhelms your
spirit.

Each winter, you observe the snow's descent,
A shroud of white enveloping the earth,
As you lament with every fleeting day,
And the agony of your loss engulfs you with its
worth.

Still, you remain by the window,
Hoping that one day she will return to you,
And the warmth of her embrace will melt the
frost within your soul.

A Father's Lament

Today, the walls bear witness to my raw truth,
Unspoken words weigh heavy in the still air,
Gathered in the depths of my wounded heart,
Snatched away by fate's cruel and callous hand,
Before you could bask in the golden rays of life.
This moment scorches my soul, a branding iron,
Etching an indelible, unwanted tattoo of regret,
A haunting reminder of the day my pride
crumbled,
My sacred duty to bestow upon you love
untamed.
But instead, you ascended to the heavens too
early, Leaving my paternal arms bereft and
weeping.
Now, these walls stand as stalwart confidants,
Witnesses to the ebb and flow of seasons' dance,
From the blossoming of spring to summer's
blaze,
Fall's descent with its solemn hues, winter's bite,
A ceaseless cycle echoing the reminder of your
absence, A void that haunts my very being, with
no respite. May you find eternal solace, sweet
child of mine,
For with each passing day, I am consumed,

By a silent demise that torments my shattered
soul,
A specter of darkness, a tempest that defies time.

Labyrinth of Despair

Oh, simple things, lost in the depths of time
Where have you vanished, free spirits sublime?
My hours trickle away, yearning for a tether,
A respite to cling to, before surrendering
altogether.
Tell me, when shall I dance in your embrace,
Where moments grant me solace and a fresh
pace?
I implore you, reveal a sign, a beacon's light.
For in this prolonged abyss, my spirit takes
flight.
Long have I dwelled in the depths of despair,
Joy's allure fading, leaving me threadbare,
Needing refuge for this weary soul I bear,
Oh, simple things, restore my love affair.
Lost in the labyrinth of my own skin
Unrequited longing fuels the pain within.
These scars etched upon my arm so deep,
A desperate plea to feel once more, to keep.

A Voice For the Voiceless

Within twilight's clasp, secrets find repose,
I rise, herald of the silent, refined, adorned in
regal prose.
The voiceless discover solace upon my stage,
A symphony of liberation, fears forever
assuaged.

In a world enfeebled by its own cacophony,
I awaken, savaging apathy's monotony.
The powerless beckon, their chains I dismantle,
Their silenced cries emancipated, no more to
trample.

As sentinel, I stand tall, embracing their plight,
Bearing their burdens with grace, carrying their
fight.
My voice, sharpened steel; my words, an
unyielding fortress,
Whispered strength, empowering them to
progress.

In creatures' anguish, the sparrow's melodious
wail,
Resonates through the silence, unveils a
triumphant tale.

In this muted symphony, I surge, unyielding,
Charting the unspoken, a champion never
yielding.

The once-blind world now compelled to hear,
Listening, comprehending, the voiceless' spirit
they revere.
I am the warrior amidst strife, guardian of hope's
thrall,
Proclaiming stories of valor, fighting for justice
with each call.

Across life's vast expanse, I vow with solemn
might,
A testament of resilience, a beacon shining
bright.
Injustices of old overturned, vanquished by our
flame,
A clarion call resounds, a torch that shall forever
proclaim.

www.ingramcontent.com/pod-product-compliance
Lightning Source LLC
LaVergne TN
LVHW021306200726
843509LV00012B/1801